Distributed by:

soundconcepts
creative business solutions

782 S. Auto Mall Dr., Suite A
American Fork, UT 84003
IsaSalesTools.com

IMPORTANT NOTICE

DISCLAIMER

Although the information contained in this book was prepared from
sources that are believed to be accurate and reliable, the publisher
strongly advises readers to seek the advice of their personal health care
professional(s) before proceeding with any changes in any health
care program.

Table of Contents

Foreword

Words of advice are a perilous gift, no matter who writes them. Language paints a meager picture of reality and all courses may run ill.

To tip the scale in favor all I can give you is my word that the trust of those I love is held in what I write.

I lean heavily on the wisdom of leaders whom many scholars consider the greatest of all time. In this small book I can include only a few of them to illustrate the development of humanity that led to the system of Quiet Mind. I hope they inspire you to a life of constant joy and love that enhances the great work of improving our civilization for everyone.

May it light you in dark places when other lights go out.

Michael Colgan
May 2013

1
Emotional Distress

Skin, hair, clothes, and disposition blending shades of grey, Mae slept for warmth on the air grate in the footpath by my apartment in Manhattan. When first I proffered a croissant, feet lashed out acompanied by a string of curses. Mae's memories of homeless life in the city distorted her emotional response to all encounters.

Over several months I got to know her. Sharing coffee and croissants on the stoop, Mae told me of two children, a happy urban home, and the sudden death of her husband, creating emotional and financial disaster that left her alone on the street.

City folk share similar demons of despair.

Though medicated for depression, Mae's speech affirmed her high intelligence and college-educated former life, where she held a banking job before her marriage. But she had become so fearful and enraged at her homeless, penniless condition that punishing herself for it seemed the only thing she could do.

Mae was not in pain or physically ill. The City had taken her children only after she ran out of money and emotional strength to care for them. She was driven to the streets by demons created in her own mind.

We all share similar urban demons. Look as people on a bus, a subway train, walking in the street. Grim. My 9:00 am graduate class usually look as if they just collectively swallowed a spider. Few seem to be rejoicing at the wondrous gift of life.

Colgan 2013

*Urban centers of higher education are raging hells
of emotional stress for the unprepared.*

Mindless choice of time and place that leaves you seething in snarled traffic is a prime example of the emotional grip of urban rage. Rushing to an airport only to find a cancelled flight that could have been checked on your phone, breeds angst beyond control in folk who fail to impose essential order on their days. Fender benders on the street their child must walk to school cause never-ending angst in mothers who have let themselves be shaped by circumstance into that place.

In his play, *SubUrbia,* in which unthinking city folk fall victim to urban turmoil, playwright Eric Bogosian sums up their powerless angst :

"It's my duty as a human being to be pissed off".

Do not waste one precious day that way. Use the knowledge herein to arrange your life with calm and steadfast purpose to live in joy and love. It is worth memorizing the words of renowned philosopher Osho:

"Misery is really hard work; that's why it makes you look so tired. Our natural state is bliss." - Osho

2

Urban Demons Rule

Cities are cruel environments for human DNA. Beneath the bustle of our lives, beat hearts of hunter-gatherers attuned to empty plains.

For at least six million years, our human genes evolved in a sparsely populated but treacherous environment, where honed emotions of fear and anger spiked instant energy to fight or flee. Those most skilled at using these emotions survived to be our ancestors.

The five thousand years of human civilization is far too short a time to change our DNA. Ancient defenses of fear and anger reside unchanged in structures of our brain. They become emotional problems whenever culture triggers them, yet forbids the use of their instant energy in vigorous fight or flight.

It's easy to see how urban snarl intensifies our angst. The squeeze of city life cuts personal space to inches, privacy to locks and blinds.

Manufacturers dictate the shapes and functions of our household goods and chattels, and what fashions we must wear, forms of ugliness so intense we have to change them every year,

Passing fads of correctness hobble language. Politicians mandate morality. Media usurp truth. Insurance companies control health care. Entrepreneurs contrive the arts. Justice is dispensed by erudite but empty men.

In tiny unconnected pools of influence, thousands of bureaucrats dicker away unknown to each other, grabbing whatever they can, in a culture grown too complex for ordinary minds.

Head down with make-work busyness at rules and forms and fees, the grumpy clerk pontificates as he accepts my check,

> *"Failing to sort your garbage into the right color bins put out on the right days, (Sundays and Holidays excepted) is a crime punishable by the fine stated and other penalties (dismemberment implied for three strikes out)."*

Reminds me of Ratty's poem in Wind in the Willows:

> *"All along the backwater,*
> *Through the rushes tall,*
> *Ducks are a-dabbling,*
> *Up tails all!"*

Do not get caught in sightless bureaucracy. Avoid it and everyone in it by all the means you can. Life is too precious to spend one hour in bureaucratic toil. Adopt the program herein and design each day to live as you desire, purposefully in passion and joy. Then even city life becomes a great adventure.

Ducks a-dabbling. Sightless bureaucracy. Leave it for the birds.

3
Medication Fails

Like my homeless friend Mae, more than 45 million people in the United States and Canada are so emotionally distressed they take antidepressant drugs every day. Use of antidepressants more than tripled in North America between 1990 and 2005.

One in every ten people you see walking down the mall, now takes daily drugs to mask the symptoms of negative emotions. The World Health Organization predicts that, by 2020, emotional disorder will grow to become the second leading cause of disability in North America, second only to heart disease.

Antidepressants provide a short-term chemical straightjacket that relieves emotional symptoms by numbing the brain, just as Novocain numbs the pain of an abscessed tooth. Overall, however, they are ineffective. Like Novocain, they mask the pain but do naught to cure the ill.

Serotonin-reuptake-inhibitors (SRIs) have become the legal drug of choice, even though reviews show only moderate benefits, and a devastating rise in risk of suicide among those using them. Medical journals suggest these drugs are improving, and we should keep an open mind. As a medical scientist for the last 50 years, my best advice about the improving face of medicine is: **Do not keep your mind so open that your brain falls out.**

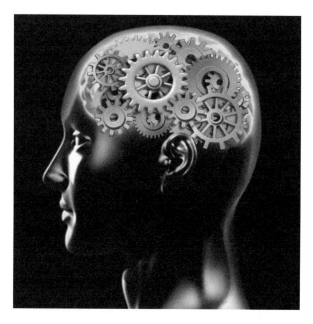

Emotional cogs that grind in the mind
cannot be fixed with medication.

You cannot cure fear, anger, depression, hatred, grief, melancholy or any negative emotion with drugs, surgery, or other medical intervention, because they are rooted in your memory and triggered by your environment. You can cure them only by making changes to your mind.

It's difficult to make these changes by yourself. Most of us need a system and a guide. I want to share with you our method, which has enabled many people to remove emotional distress from their lives. To change your brain towards joy is far more valuable to your health and well-being, than any medical treatment, any doctor, any drug, any other approach to life that I know. We call it, **Quiet Mind.**

How do you begin? In the *Tao of Pooh,* Benjamin Hoff gives simple but potent advice well worth remembering:

> *"If you really want to be happy, you can begin by appreciating who you are and what you've got."*

AA Milne's effortlessly, calm, and joyful Winnie the Pooh.

> *"But you could be doing something important."*
> *"I am", said Pooh.*
> *"Oh? Doing what?"*
> *"Listening to the ducks."*

4
Banish Anger

Physical danger does not happen much in our civilized society. Most events that warp emotions are not physically damaging and require no action to thwart them. Yet many folk allow the instinctive emotion of anger to explode over trifles, such as burning the toast or someone usurping your position in a line.

Here's a key to help you overcome needless anger.

Whenever little things make you angry, they are telling you the size of who you are.

Many folk are unaware of their needless anger at the most innocuous twaddle. At morning coffee break one of my academic colleagues regularly becomes furious at his pet peeve, senseless bureaucracy, which he calls an "idiocracy". Face reddening with rage, his legs fall open like a door so his paunch can tremble freely as he vents. Whenever you allow anything to make you angry in this way, it is plundering your self-control.

Few sights are more ludicrous than an enraged golfer thrashing the ball because it obstinately refuses to go in the hole.

I suggested he should write furious letters to the offenders to let the anger out. He seemed mollified until I also told him never to mail them. No wonder he's on medication for hypertension and heart disease.

Some folk get angry immediately if anyone is angry with them. Acting coaches teach politicians to pretend to be furious in this way, so as to appear more powerful and concerned. As we see every day, most of them are really bad actors, and never get past the spoiled child level.

Whole cultures, however, especially those on the financial and educational edge, respond habitually with real anger at each other for even a snarky word out of place. The rate of Alzheimer's among these people is very high, and their lifespan short – and likely miserable. Any time you get angry at someone's angry words, you are allowing them to offload their anger onto you. It benefits no one, and damages your brain besides.

Constrained rage seldom results in the vigorous physical action necessary to dissipate the energy and relieve the distress. That's why counting to ten doesn't work so well. Far better to do 100 pushups. It dissipates the energy, gives you healthy exercise and may be the only time you can make 100.

Anger management has become almost a fashion in our elbow-to-elbow society. Germany has just opened the first abuse hotline (Schimpfhotline) where (for a fee) angry people can scream and swear for 15 minutes at some anonymous poor soul paid to listen. Schimpfhotline is now running non-stop 16 hours a day and expanding fast.

In Russia urban family fights have become so bad that some talk show hosts suggest venting your anger verbally on complete strangers in the street, rather than on your wife and children.

Better for consuming the energy of rage is the Japanese system of mannequins that resemble company management. After work, angry employees can go and beat the comeuppance out of the mannequins with sponge rubber clubs. But if you have to resort to any of these ploys, it's likely time for professional help.

Never bottle it. Bottled anger is destructive only for the person who rages, never for those who calmly witness the rage. In my book, Save Your Brain, I analyze research showing how bottled rage damages the brain.

It's worth remembering how Buddha put it 2,500 years ago:

*"You may not be punished for your anger,
but you will be punished by it."*

Never let it stew. There is wisdom in the old saying, *"Don't let the sun go down upon your anger"*. Much better to stay up and fight until you are both over it. If it ends in mutual shame and canoodling you got it right.

You may not be punished for your anger,
but you will be punished by it.

Begin today to take these steps to banish anger from your life:

1. **Become AWARE of needless anger**. Simply becoming aware is halfway to eliminating it. Allowing yourself to become angry is self-punishment. For every minute of needless anger you lose a minute of joy you will never get again.

2. **Acknowledge the destructive effects of anger on your brain** and resolve to prevent them. Banish anger to prevent Alzheimer's: it's an easy decision.

3. **Realize you always have the choice to become angry or not.** The instant you allow anger to rise in any controversy, you have stopped seeking a solution and started indulging your ego. Each time you choose to remain calm, instead, you take a step closer to reason and joy.

4. **Never react instantly with anger**. Use your reason to assess whether or not the situation is a physical threat. If not, focus instead on what all of us want to achieve: life's wondrous journey of joy.

5
Conquer Fear

Fear is an ancient response of the brain to perceived threat. In moderate amounts it protects us by making us more careful. We may even incite moderate fear for the thrill, as folk do with fairground rides. At age 14, my youngest sister used to beg me repeatedly to take her to the midnight horror movies. She then spent the show alternately screaming and burying her face in my arm.

Large fear reactions, however, differ in quality not just in amount from thrill fear, and can cause serious illness.

Strong fear that is not dissipated quickly builds up excitatory chemicals in the brain to damaging levels. These chemicals puncture cell membranes, causing chemical leaks, and forming a deadly free radical called peroxynitrite.

Fear also increases heart rate and blood pressure, disrupts balance and bowel function, and can render the sufferer unable to speak or move ("rooted to the spot"). Persistent fear reactions can continue for weeks or months rendering the sufferer helpless, and inevitably damaging the brain.

Paralyzing fear can even knock you unconscious or cause a heart attack and kill you. There are numerous records of executions by witchdoctors in undeveloped societies, by simply pointing a bone that literally scares the victim to death. Bone pointing executions by ritual killers called Kurdaicha still occur in Northern Australia.

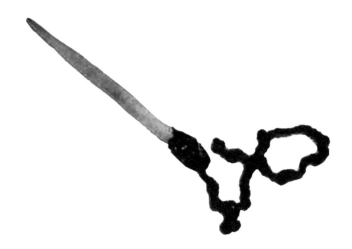

Bone used in Australian ritual bone-pointing that kills by fear alone. Stolen hair of victim is glued to the end.

We are all subject to similar manipulations of the mind. Western countries abound in ghosts and demons, and exorcisms are still performed by clergy, including one by the Bishop of Monmouth in Wales in 2012. In scientific studies, cool water can raise real burns if the victim is led to fear it is boiling.

Yet fear does not exist in any object or situation. It has no physical existence at all. **Fear is purely an emotional construction that you create in your own mind.**

Begin today to take three steps to remove fear from your life:

1. Whenever you become afraid, use this reminder: **"There I go again, frightening myself "**.

2. Face diluted situations of your fears. A brilliant student of mine was so afraid of public speaking he would be struck dumb and trembling and have to leave the stage. I started removing his fear by having him do talks to just me in an empty lecture hall. Over several months we added people until he could speak to a full room. Now he lectures calmly to international audiences. **Practice preventing fear in diluted situations of your worst fears. Make diluted fear your friend and the full fear will disappear.**

3. Fear has many instinctive bodily expressions, including covering the eyes, screaming, crouching, trembling, turning away, sharp intakes of breath, and paralysis of motor movement. **To prevent fear developing, avoid its instinctive expressions by doing the opposite. Stand erect, silent, square your shoulders, relax your muscles, breathe deeply and evenly as detailed in Chapter 9. Smile, face your fear and stride directly and purposely towards it. Even if you are initially terrified, when you do what you fear repeatedly, death of that fear is certain.**

Many folk don't realize the tremendous bonus you get from facing fears. Face one fear repeatedly until you conquer it, and the courage generalizes to other fears. Other unthinkable actions become within your grasp. Overcome your fear of talking to strangers and the impossible walk along the cliff-top edge becomes a pleasant stroll. Overcome the stage fright of speaking alone to an audience, and the previously impossible bungee jump can become a laughing leap. What power our brains have if only we take the initial scary steps.

6
Senses Distort Experience

Thoughts invade the mind at such a rapid rate, we give each one barely time to recognize its passing. Some of these thoughts excite emotional circuits in the brain that reverberate long after the event that triggered them is forgotten. Consequently, numerous negative emotional memories of fear and anger may persist for years, yet are not attached in memory to any concrete situation.

A lifelong fear of insects for example, can follow a single forgotten experience of a spider crawling up your nose. Given the environmental stimulus of an insect close by, negative emotional memories from the forgotten spider can trigger ancient fear circuits in the mid-brain.

"Father of Stress", Dr. Hans Selye showed decades ago how these circuits fire autonomic nerves that control our housekeeping functions, from heartbeat and blood pressure, to gut reactions, trembling, and bowel movements. Because of a long established emotional trigger—a trigger that may be no longer conscious—a harmless stimulus can be misperceived as danger, leaving the person terrified and nauseous.

I have outlined three strategies to protect you from such fears. Whenever you are afraid, it is most important to be instantly aware that you have frightened yourself. Knowing that fear does not exist in any situation but is only a construction built in your own mind, is halfway to eliminating it.

Anger is worse than fear. Many folk stoutly defend their right to be angry at any time, especially in response to anger from others. They are unaware that the damage created by the anger is mostly to their own brain. Simply becoming aware of needless anger is halfway to preventing it. Life without anger greatly increases joy.

Sensory Distortion

The next step on our journey is to realize that what you see is never what you get. Our senses distort everything we see, hear, touch, taste, and smell. To remove negative emotional memories from your brain, you need to accept that the normal human brain operates by constant distortion of sensory input.

I will use the sense of vision because it is easiest to illustrate in a book. The same applies to all our senses. The sights and sounds of horror movies, such as the Freddy Krueger series, are designed effectively to incite all the mental and bodily changes of fear, even though the audience knows they are only films with ghoulish make-up and fake sound, and cannot jump out of the screen to get you.

My first visual example is movement. The impossible movement shown in the stationary picture is an example of the sensory distortion that occurs in vision 24 hours a day. You cannot stop it. This movement is similar to the distortion of emotions by triggering negative emotional memories in the brain, memories whose causes are long forgotten.

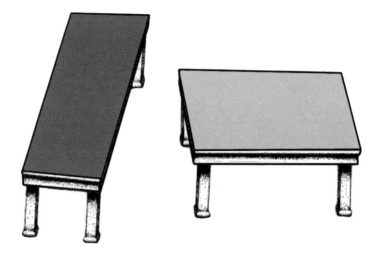

The next example is perceived size. The two tables shown are exactly the same length and width, but our eyes see them as very different from each other. Hard to believe? Take a ruler and measure them.

This visual distortion is similar to an irrational fear, a situation perceived as fearful even though there is no threat. To eliminate such irrational fears is a difficult task unless you use the right method. **Quiet Mind,** provides a reliable path.

The third example is perceived angle. Our eyes see the blue lines on the next page at angles to each other. In fact they are exactly parallel.

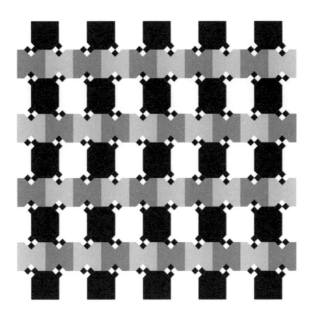

A fourth example is color. The two horses in the picture below are exactly the same color, but our eyes see one of them as yellow and the other as reddish brown. To prove it to yourself take a sheet of paper and cut two small holes to expose part of each horse simultaneously.

With just these simple examples you can see that visual experience of movement, size, angle, and color are all distorted by the actions of our brain.

Whenever you are confused by what you see, it is worth remembering the words of Antoine de St Exupery from *The Little Prince:*

"On ne voit bien qu'avec le cœur. L'essentiel est invisible pour les yeux."
("One sees clearly only with the heart. The essential is invisible to the eyes.")

There is one crucial difference between sensory distortions and distorted emotions. Sensory distortions are an unchangeable part of our brain structure. Emotional distortions, however, are all learned, and thus, with the right program, can be unlearned.

Afraid of making the change? Remember, you will be changed anyway at the whims of time and circumstance. And time is never gentle. Unless you direct the changes you become an emotional puppet of chance.

Change yourself deliberately or be changed willy-nilly. Take a cue from Bilbo in J.R.R. Tolkien's *Lord of the Rings:*

"It's a dangerous business, Frodo, going out your front door.
You step onto the road, and if you don't keep your feet,
there's no knowing where you might be swept off to."

Afraid to try? Our biggest fear of making positive change is fear of failure, failure that will leave us sadder and more disheartened, and likely ashamed of our weakness. To help overcome this fear, reformulate failures as opportunities. Don't vacillate; don't dither. Decide firmly, then act with all your being. All great leaders act passionately to push the limits until they break, failing many time before succeeding. Failure liberates success.

My friend, famous ambassador of success, Jimmy Smith, gave me the key. You should memorize his subtle wisdom:

"Learn to love your failures. Embrace them. Every "No" is one step closer to a "Yes". - Jimmy Smith

Several folk have said to me well, that just probability. You ask enough people and you are bound to get a "Yes" eventually.

No way. Jimmy "the Butcher" is a lot wiser than that. The main advantage of embracing repeated failures is that they train your brain to do it right.

Michael Jordan, likely the best NBA player of all time, knows well the necessity of failure:

"I have missed more than 9,000 shots in my career. I have lost almost 300 games. On 26 occasions I have been entrusted to take the game winning shot, and missed. I have failed over and over and over again in my life. And that is why I succeed."

How do you begin? Start today to become AWARE of yourself and your needless negative emotions about failure. If past failures, or tender ego make you hesitant, consider Buddha's wise words:

"By your own efforts waken yourself, watch yourself.
And live joyfully. You are the master."

Similar wisdom is given by Lao Tzu in the *Tao Te Ching:*

"The key to growth is the introduction of higher dimensions of
consciousness into our awareness."

Will you succeed? Yes Indeed. Remember this deceptively simple but profound quote about persistence from Dr. Seuss in *Oh, The Places You'll Go:*

"And will you succeed? Yes indeed, yes indeed! Ninety-eight
and three quarters percent guaranteed !" - Dr. Seuss

7
From Melancholy
To Joy

Our goal herein is to develop a quiet and loving mind for life's journey of joy. Financial gain and material goods, for which many trade their lives, are trivial by comparison. Despite endless commercial urging, do not confuse standard of living with quality of life.

Although we spend most of our lives working for it, money is only a means to develop joy within yourself, your family, and those around you. Many studies show that, beyond a certain minimum, which varies with costs of food and shelter in different places, more money does not lead to greater joy.

Marketing guru Michael S. Clouse

As my friend, marketing guru Michael Clouse, says, if you dread Mondays and long for Fridays, ask the person you see in the mirror what they think they are doing wasting your life. If you are saddened by your work, you have only one life in which to change it, and you must lead the change. Joyless work is only for the beaten. Clever people play.

The Dalai Lama has great material wealth and high public position, yet lives a life of joy and love as a simple monk. Mahatma Gandhi had no material wealth, and never held a public position, and lived a life of joy and love as a simple monk. Both are revered leaders worldwide because, despite material things or lack of them, they embody a life of joy, and spread love to everyone around them.

Absorb the words of the Dalai Lama:

"The greatest purpose of work is to foster joy." - The Dalai Lama

If your past life has been unhappy, emotional memories of negative experiences accumulate to form an underlying tone of melancholy. Melancholy promotes fear, anger, hatred, physical and mental illness, and premature aging. Each of us operates habitually at some point between the poles of joy and melancholy.

Melancholy makes difficult any enduring steps to change it. The more you fan the coal of anger the hotter it burns. The deeper you hide from fear, the darker it shadows you. The higher you climb the mountain of regret, the higher it grows.

You cannot achieve **Quiet Mind** by tomorrow afternoon, but you do not have to become a monk to do it. You do not have to give up anything nor even the desire for it.

What you have to change is what I call the "Teddy Bear Syndrome", clinging to material things as if they will protect you from the boogey man. Begin instead to act deliberately every day to foster joy within yourself in everything you do.

"Now that I've freed myself from desire for material things, how do I free myself from the desire to be free from desire for material things?"

It's not easy. Each step you try to take outside your habitual emotional zone is like giving up a teddy bear. Negative emotional memories assume the shapes of many demons before you can eliminate them. To reach the morning, you have to pass these shadows of the night.

It takes more than fashionable psychological counseling, pungent herbal baths, head tapping, or positive affirmations, such as the popular, "I must, I must be humorous". But many folk will pay for any poppycock, no matter the cost, before ever considering they have to face themselves and make the changes from within.

Inner changes are made more difficult by our materialistic culture, which conditions us to believe that a joyful life first requires the scrabbling pursuit of material goals, by means that are often at odds with truth, honor, and integrity.

"Nothing personal, just business." Is the ritual excuse.

These "Bisy Backsons" (Busy. Back Soon) as Pooh calls them in Benjamin Hoff's *Tao of Pooh,* convince themselves that material success and joy are synonymous. They see both waiting together, always just down the road, just around the next turn, up the next step, each quickly discarded for the next and the next. Pooh sums them up much better than I:

"They burn their toast a lot."

Nobel Laureate Daniel Kahneman of Princeton University has shown that if everyone in the U.S. had the same access to money it would improve life satisfaction by less than 5%. He explains our lunatic drive for material things as the "focusing illusion", a deliberate ploy of marketers and politicians. They fool people to believe that every new "must-have" will bring much greater joy into their lives than it possibly can. We live in a culture where every unnecessary knickknack is somehow deemed essential.

Again, my Zen master Winnie the Pooh sums it up best:

"Although eating honey is a Very Good Thing, there is a moment just before you begin eating that is better than when you do."

Bisy Backsons are always confusing accumulation with progress. Their minds are never quiet enough to realize that most of the joy resides in the journey, not the destination.

Habitually joyful people are no more special nor gifted than most. They simply realize that the journey of life is purely for joy. They accept that joy requires a pure and honest mind, and that they have to achieve it within themselves. They understand that the only emotions that yield constant joy are unconditional love and compassion. And they practice them—every day.

You can do it too. Nothing in your past actually affects the present. What you see as the past is simply memory traces in the brain of a former version of you. Do not allow them to dictate a moment of your life. Now, this present moment, has never happened before. It is fresh and pure, unsullied. Seize it with all your being to create the masterpiece of joy that waits within you.

"Although eating hunny is a Very Good Thing, there is a moment just before you begin eating that is better than when you do."

8
The Weakness
of Deceit

If you habitually deceive others, it is inevitable that you will come to deceive yourself. Self-deception renders **Quiet Mind** difficult to achieve. Here I do not write of softening your words for kindness, nor enriching them to enhance someone's joy, but of lies told to gain advantage or avoid censure.

Deceit for advantage is widely tolerated, even applauded, in our society. It's the cornerstone of *The Apprentice,* one of the most popular shows on television It has become such an accepted vehicle of promotion and marketing that few people believe anything that appears in an advertisement.

Marketing lies, however, influence all of us. Many folk feel they have to match them in their own lives just to keep up and appear greater, or more interesting, or more fun, than they are. In doing so, they squander their own credibility. As Einstein said:

"Whosoever is careless with truth in small things cannot be trusted with important matters."

Worse, in the depth of the heart of any intelligent person, each lie places an emotional burden of shame and guilt. As the burden grows, their self-integrity diminishes, until deceit becomes the habit of their life, and truth for them is indistinguishable from fiction. In such a state, **Quiet Mind** and life's blissful journey of joy are forever beyond them.

My erstwhile homeless friend Mae in Chapter 1 lives today in assisted housing, and has a bookkeeping job and access to her children. Step by tiny step she relinquished her life of self-deceit. Her high intelligence and education helped only a little to find the way. The medication she took to mask emotional pain likely reduced her progress. But she began to face herself and live the truth every day and gradually recovered her capacity for joy.

All you really have in life is your body and your word. To compromise either to gain advantage or avoid blame, even in little things, retards your progress on life's journey of joy.

Adopting a life of truth may seem a massive task, and may seem to put you at a disadvantage in our culture. But, even a few steps along the way the power of truth to enrich you and those around you becomes apparent. Embrace truth in word and action and you will shine like a beacon in our ocean of deceit. As Gandhi said,

> *"If you can do anything with purity of spirit, it is so rare in our society it cannot help but make a difference."*

9
Origins of Quiet Mind

You can't jump straight into **Quiet Mind.** .Heed Confucius:

> *"The mechanic who would perfect his*
> *work must first sharpen his tools."*

When you first take up the path, you have to sharpen the tools you need to achieve a mental state which reveals negative emotional baggage for what it is — destructive memories of fear, anxiety, anger, hatred, shame guilt, regret, and grief, from your past. Just as you have placed each of these memories in the circuits of your brain, sharp tools will enable you to cut them out.

After more than 20 years research, our method has come to focus on the most ancient philosophical texts, called the Vedas. Very briefly, these are the earliest profound writings to explain the nature of reality, and the form and method of human self-realization.

"The mechanic who would perfect his work must first sharpen his tools." - Confucius

The Vedas were compiled by many different authors in a mix of ancient Indo-European languages from about 3,000 B.C., over a large area from Northern India, to Egypt, to Phoenicia (now Lebanon). In various forms they spread to China and throughout India, and profoundly influenced the development of Buddhism.

Through incorporation of the Vedas into the later Upanishads written in Sanskrit, and later again into the great book, *The Bhagavad Gita,* they also formed the basis of Hindu philosophy.

Copies of the Vedas spread to Greece from whence they became the source of most Western philosophies today. After Greek society was overrun by Rome, Roman derivations written in Greek by Greek scholars became the basis for Rome's development of the Christian Gospels.

Many changes in these philosophies made to suit different times, cultures and rulers, have left only remnants of the original wisdom. Fortunately, the rules under which they were originally written remain the same. The Universe, including us, operates serenely under the exact mathematical laws of its creation, laws that are unaffected by the details of any particular liturgy.

Quiet Mind leans most towards the simplest form we can find of the ancient philosophies as it occurs in Zen Buddhism. "Zen" is not Japanese in origin. It is derived from the Sanskrit "Dyana" which developed in India after the birth of Siddhartha Gautama in 563 B.C. in what is now Nepal. Renamed Buddha, which means "Awakened", he founded Buddhism.

Over the next millennium, the Buddhist sect grew rapidly. It spread to Pakistan, Tibet and China, where Dyana was translated into Chinese as "Ch'an".

First century manuscripts of Buddhism, written in one of the most ancient languages, Kharoshthi script, on birchbark scrolls, were found at Gandhara in Pakistan in the 1990s. Part of one of the scrolls is pictured on the next page. They have since been translated by British and American scholars to give us the earliest, and likely most accurate, rendition of Buddha's teachings. We use these translations for our program **Quiet Mind**.

Fragment of first-century birchbark scrolls of Buddha's teachings found in Gandhara in Pakistan in the 1990s.

Since at least the 12th century, Japanese practitioners of Buddhism have followed two main methods of advancement. The Soto sect (Farmer Zen) favors regular meditation to promote a gradual dawning of insight. The Rinzai sect (Warrior Zen) favors flashes of insight that occur by regular contemplation of koans (apparently illogical statements). Both sects agree on the necessity to achieve a quiet mind, which they call *"mushin"*. The best I can do to explain it in English is; a mind free from artifice, distraction, obstruction, and inhibition.

It bears remembering: **a mind free from artifice, distraction, obstruction, and inhibition.**

Stone head of Buddha, 3rd century, Pakistan

"The way is not in the sky. The way is in the heart." - Buddha

The central practice of Zen, called *"zazen"*, involves sitting for a period each day in meditation. From our experience with thousands of athletes, and folk who come to the Colgan Institute seeking answers to aging and ill health, we know that zazen is difficult for many people raised in Western culture.

Most of us are conditioned by our culture to crave external stimulation. We are taught to revere busy-ness, and to live under the pervading illusion of modern life that solutions to problems can be found immediately, like instant mashed potato or instant coffee. To sit, apparently doing nothing, seems appropriate only for the old. In the 1990s, we resolved to find a way that better fits our culture.

Over the past 20 years, we have developed a method of contemplation more appropriate to Western lives. We teach people to meditate while busily in action, doing solitary, repetitive, skilled tasks, tasks that may require little conscious thought, but which have no limit to the skill you can attain. Examples include, tending a garden, doing carpentry, or practicing a sport such as archery or golf, or exercising in a defined way. We have developed the method to complement exercising in the Colgan Power Program, and use that as the illustration herein.

Though symbols may suit other approaches to self-realization, **Quiet Mind** does not need any special chant or sound or other symbol. We have long accepted the wisdom of the founders of Taoism, compiled as the writings of Lao Tzu, written more than 2,500 years ago:

"Chanting is no more holy than listening to the murmur of a stream, counting prayer beads no more sacred than breathing, religious robes no more spiritual than work clothes." - Lao Tzu

Ancient painting of Lao Tzu leaving civilization for mountain solitude.

Our goal is to develop your ability to step back from the body and realize that life is inherently a daily adventure of joy. You then become immune to most of the negative emotions that control the majority of people. You gain the capacity to attach joy, love and compassion to almost any event.

You will find that the best of life is in communicating your joy in love to everyone around you, both those who love you and those who don't. As Jesus said:

"Love thine enemies, do good to those who hate you, bless those who curse you, pray for those who abuse you." (Luke 6:27-32)

10
Quiet Mind 1
Three-Part Breath

At the first level of **Quiet Mind**, you learn to use what we call Three-Part Breath with each repetition of your chosen task. Initially it is not easy. Progress comes only from constantly doing it. *"There is no try. Either do or do not." - Yoda, Star Wars: The Empire Strikes Back*

At rest, healthy people take about 15 breaths a minute. That is 900 breaths every hour, over 20,000 breaths every day. The form, rhythm, and timing of the breath influence every movement we make.

Yet most of the people who come to the Colgan Institute breathe badly. The major faults are:

1. Shallow, top-of-chest breathing,

2. Exhaling at the point of effort,

3. Breathing uncoordinated with movement.

For many people, top-of-chest breathing is all they do. They never properly oxygenate their muscles or their brain. Yet they often wonder why they fatigue easily, and become emotionally fragile. Just think how bad any other skilled movement would be if you did it so incorrectly 20,000 times a day.

To remind yourself to focus on the breath habitually here are the words of world renowned Zen master Thich Nhat Hanh, from his book *Stepping into Freedom:*

"Feelings come and go like clouds in a windy sky. Conscious breathing is my anchor." - Zen Master Thich Nhat Hahn

Start today to optimize your breath and thereby increase the flow of oxygen and nutrients to the brain. Breathe and exercise each day as Nature designed us to breathe and exercise, and eat the organic, living food that Nature designed us to eat. After a short while your physical and mental health will soar.

You need to practice **Quiet Mind** for 30 minutes each day. Use good music to help you get an even breathing rhythm. In his book, *This is Your Brain on Music,* my colleague Daniel Levitin at McGill University shows clearly how music is built into the structure of the human brain. .

Remember, throughout the world, babies in the uterus respond to music with better growth and health. And diverse peoples who speak hundreds of different languages, all have the same musical scale.

As great violinist Yehudi Menuhin says:

"Music is inherent in every human being – a birthright."

Ravi Shankar's superb sitar will help you get your breathing rhythm.

Three-Part Breath

You must get the breath right first, before you can progress further. Morning before eating is the best time to practice. Together with your chosen task, focus on excellence of the breath, its structure, rhythm, and timing, and its coordination with your movement.

First, and most important, inhale into the lower third of your lungs, the area most richly endowed with oxygen receptors. The easiest way to learn is to pull the diaphragm down by sticking the belly out, the relaxed "belly breathing" taught in yoga for at least 3,000 years.

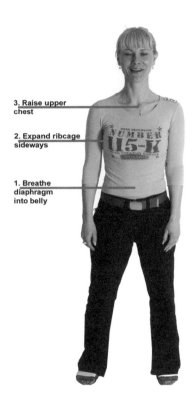

3. Raise upper chest

2. Expand ribcage sideways

1. Breathe diaphragm into belly

Three Part Breath

Second, fill the middle third of the lungs by expanding your ribcage sideways. Get a friend to place their fingers on the sides of your ribs just below the shoulder blades. They should be able to feel the ribcage widen by at least two inches.

Third, fill the top of your lungs by raising the chest. Then pause the full breath for one second.

Exhale in the reverse order. Empty the top of the lungs, then narrow the ribcage, then pull in the stomach. Then pause one second again.

Breathing this way you receive the most oxygen per breath. After some practice, the three parts of the breath and the inhalation and exhalation become one smooth sequence, and the pauses a slowing and reversal.

The next major fault we see is exhalation at the point of effort during exercise. This practice arose partly because insurance companies learned that holding the breath at the point of effort increases intra-abdominal pressure, raises blood pressure, and puts unfit people at risk. Consequently, mainly for insurance purposes, average gym clients are taught to exhale as they make an effort. No elite athlete we have trained ever breathes in this way.

It is true that retained breath on effort raises intra-abdominal pressure. That is exactly how evolution programmed the body. Intra-abdominal pressure stabilizes the core. That is why you inhale sharply as a reflex when faced with a sudden threat. Our ancient fight-flight system triggers the body to inhale to stabilize the core, to make you as strong and integrated as possible for fighting or fleeing.

In **Quiet Mind**, we take advantage of this superb reflex to apply maximum power for minimum effort. You inhale immediately before effort, and momentarily retain the breath during a rapid concentric contraction of a movement (when the muscles are shortening under load). Then you release the breath evenly during a slow eccentric contraction (when the muscles are lengthening again).

It takes between 40 and 100 daily 30-minute sessions to learn Three Part Breath.

Breathe in rhythmic coordination with movement.

11
Quiet Mind 2 Movement

Once you have learned to breathe easily, you shift focus. At the second level of **Quiet Mind**, as you make each movement of your chosen task for 30 minutes each day, focus your whole mind on that movement alone. Exclude everything else to focus intently on every moment of the movement with your full awareness.

We chose resistance exercise as our vehicle for Quiet Mind because its clear relation to health has made it a prime choice of leaders throughout history. You can find the details of our exercise program on www. colganinstitute.com. Many leaders today recommend similar daily exercise as essential for the mind as well as the body. It came from a much earlier source:

"To keep the body in good health is a duty...otherwise we shall not be able to keep our mind strong and clear." - **Buddha**

Perfect, aware, balance

Whatever task you choose, you need full awareness. Test your own level of awareness now. If you cannot remember the Japanese names for the two main Zen sects given earlier, then you were not reading with awareness. You are not ready to read anything further. You should go back to the beginning of the book and start again, but this time read with *AWARENESS*.

As your awareness grows, you begin to realize that each time you act without it you waste a portion of your life that you will never get again.

As you progress in **Quiet Mind**, realization dawns slowly that the past is composed only of memories of thought, the future only of conjecture from those memories.

The past and the future are merely thoughts. They exist only in the present moment. Understand space and all we have is here. Understand time and all we have is now.

We are always and only here and now. And all that exists here and now is your mind. Use it with full awareness.

You do not need an iron will or extreme effort. To approach the **Quiet Mind** practice in a boot camp manner takes you away from the simplicity you seek, and will slow your progress.

The quieter you become, the more you will learn, and the faster you will progress. As I learned from Bruce Lee: *"Thoughts should follow their true nature and flow silently from a calm mind like water to shape and fill the form of the movement"*.

IF YOU SPEND TOO MUCH TIME THINKING ABOUT A THING, YOU'LL NEVER GET IT DONE.
BRUCE LEE

Excellence

Focus your awareness on greater and greater refinement of form in your chosen task to develop **Quiet Mind**, be it an exercise program, or gardening, or woodworking, or sports training, or art. Every session you do the task, strive for excellence.

Focus on improving some aspect of the movements; awareness, posture, timing, rhythm, coordination, balance, accuracy, relaxation, effortlessness, economy of motion, silence. Make no superfluous movement. Contract only the muscles essential to the task. With diligent practice, it will take about six months to reach Level 2 of **Quiet Mind**.

Excellence does not come by trying hard with gritted teeth as you see in many gym participants and amateur athletes. The right effort to develop excellence comes not from forcing muscles to make a movement. **The effort lies in becoming fully aware of each movement, making it a meditative act that flows from you like water.**

Perfect, relaxed, aware movement.

Excellence never occurs by mere practice. Even the wrong, practice still makes permanent. Only the right practice, focused on increasing self-awareness of the power you have within you, can make perfect.

Excellence is not a performance. It is a life habit that slowly changes your brain over a long period of repeatedly doing a task better EVERY time. It develops only by long and constant awareness.

**There is no limit to excellence in even the simplest task.
To achieve excellence in great things, you must first
make it a habit in little things.**

Shaolin head balance. Human physical abilities extend far beyond what we usually think.

12
Quiet Mind 3
The Task Does Itself

To reach Level 2 of **Quiet Mind** will take you about six months of 30 minutes each day at your chosen task, with Three-Part Breath, full awareness, and refinement of the movements. Trying to shortcut the process is like throwing yourself in the deep end of the pool before you learn to swim. Your movements in practice for **Quiet Mind** have to become as automatic as swimming movements do in children taught to swim. Before attempting Level 3, you should be able to close your eyes and still perform the movements skillfully.

If for any reason you have to miss a practice, then last thing at night visualize in detail the practice you would have done that day. Visualize every part of it, the clothes, the tools the smells, the sounds, the movements. Controlled studies with athletes and musicians, some of which are reviewed in Norman Doidge's book *The Brain That Changes Itself*, show that improvements in performance through visualization are nearly as good as actually doing the training. We always use visualization to augment our athletic training.

When you reach the level where you can close your eyes in your chosen task and allow the movements to occur, you shift your focus again. Continue to incorporate Levels 1 and 2 but now focus on performing the task with less and less effort.

Consciously relax all muscles not involved, especially those of the neck, face and expression. Gradually, you will become able to exert maximum, accurate muscular force with very little effort or movement at all. Muscle power is limited, but the power of the human mind is infinite.

The task now occurs effortlessly around your unmoving core. Your body is loose, face calm, neck relaxed, brow unfurrowed. Your mind becomes still, like a clear pool. **Consciously doing the task becomes the task doing itself. Gradually you become the silent watcher of the wonder of your own body.**

As Bruce Lee said:
"The less the effort, the faster and more powerful you will be."

Until you have this experience, it is difficult to accept that great force and accuracy can arise without conscious effort. The best short account that may help you is the much copied book, *Zen in the Art of Archery* by Eugen Herrigel. It takes some time to reach the state of *"nani mo iranu"* *(nothing is needed),* and it does not happen to the vain or idle.

Once you have reached this level, you can step back from your body and observe yourself. Your unique causes of emotional distress, the negative emotional barriers to achieving a life of joy and passion, become obvious, and progressively easier to confront and eliminate.

You begin to understand that a quiet mind is inherently a state of uncluttered simplicity. To help you achieve it, memorize the deceptively simple words of Leonardo da Vinci:

"Simplicity is the ultimate sophistication."

***Da Vinci's "Lady with an ermine" designed to the beauty
and simplicity of the Fibonacci mathematical series.***

This peaceful state of **Quiet Mind** gradually transfers from your task to any surroundings. It blocks formation of negative emotional memories from any event.

Your brain begins to register that it is not what you have, or where you are, or what you are doing, or what others are doing to you that makes you happy or unhappy, but only what you think about it. The ultimate goal is to live every moment in joyful, passionate and loving action, free from the chains of negative emotion.

Numerous controlled studies show that learning to live in this state has more beneficial effects than medication on a wide variety of disorders. These include anxiety, depression, fibromyalgia, chronic pain, asthma, inflammatory disorders of the intestines, and rheumatoid arthritis. These effects reflect large beneficial changes in the brain.

After some time in **Quiet Mind**, understanding dawns that all of life is but a meditation, a series of thoughts, to which you can attach whatever emotions you choose.

Emotional clutter empties from your mind, allowing clearer and clearer thought. Clear human thought has no bounds. Whatever great life goal you can form clearly enough in your mind you can achieve.

You Can Do It

If you do not start now, the only time you have for sure – then when? Life is too short to wait for tomorrow. The fear of Eowyn in J.R.R. Tolkien's *Return of the King*, reflects what many folk allow their lives to become:

> *"To stay behind bars, until use and old age accept them, and all chance of doing great deeds is gone beyond recall or desire."*

If you doubt your ability for even a moment read about Patrick Henry

Hughes. He was born in 1988 in Louisville, Kentucky without eyes, and unable to straighten his arms and legs, thus unable to walk. I had the pleasure of meeting him recently when he appeared at an Isagenix Convention in Phoenix.

Inspired to great purpose by his father, Patrick overcame his physical challenges. He graduated *magna cum laude* from the University of Louisville, and is now a brilliant multi-instrumental musician, singer, and motivational speaker. I have this picture of Patrick on my own motivational board.

Patrick Henry Hughes overcame great physical challenges to become a celebrated musician.

It's never too late either. After a lecture in Nanaimo, Canada in January 2013, an older lady approached the table where I was signing books. She shyly whispered she had come to hear me the year before, and resolved then at age 69 to restore her health. She said:

"Although I'm a nurse, I was very ill, in constant pain, and on five medications. I changed my head, changed my diet as you said, and hired a gym trainer. I've lost 40 lbs. I feel 1000% better. I'm 70 this year and my goal is to lose the other 30. 70 lbs off and healthy by 70 and all by the power of my own brain."

Most of us do not have severe disabilities or illness. We can get out of bed in the morning, we are not in pain, our arms work and our legs work, and we can look up and see the sky. The day is pure and new, unsullied, ready to be made the masterpiece that waits inside us. What else do we need?

To combat anyone or anything that try to hinder you on the journey to mastery, use this wisdom from Patanjali, the "Father of Yoga" who compiled the Yoga Sutras about 2,200 years ago:

"When you are inspired to some great purpose, dormant forces, faculties and talents become alive, and you discover yourself to be a greater person by far than you ever dreamed."

Yoga master BKS Iyengar at age 93 in 2011.

"Freedom and untainted bliss await you, but you have to choose to embark on the Inward Journey to discover it".

13
Select Your Friends

Those with whom you spend most time shape your thoughts. Your thoughts shape your beliefs. Your beliefs shape your actions. Your actions shape what you become. No way around it. Befriend only those who are joyful and passionate in life and you will gradually shape yourself to them.

Few of us develop sufficiently to be a Mahatma Ghandi who could live among misery and poverty and bring the people to joy. His given name was Mohandas, but he was so unaffected by circumstances around him that the people renamed him Mahatma, meaning "Great Soul".

Few of us are so far along the journey of joy that we can remain unaffected by people and situations that are joyless, that make life a problem rather than a gift to be cherished. You will see better progress if you ease your contact with the needy, the indolent, the angry, the melancholy. **You cannot become a sweet pickle in a barrel of vinegar.**

Do not allow anyone or any situation to waste your time. If you do they are stealing your life, because time is what life's made of.

Many folk have difficulty letting go. People come repeatedly to see me year after year. They are desperate to change, but continue to hang on grimly to destructive friends and habits of the past that they know are making the journey of joy impossible. They are not aware. They do not live now, in the present, the only time you have to live. They exist only as victims of the past, wasting their precious days, ever waiting for just the right circumstance to start living. Do not be one of them.

In adopting **Quiet Mind** you are removing emotional trash from your brain. It becomes much easier if you also clean house of the physical presence of people in your life who act as touchstones for negative emotions.

If it is a close situation also clean house of their material things: furniture, pictures, books, anything that reminds you of them that can act as an emotional trigger.

My friend, fitness guru Cathy Savage, puts it aptly:

> *"Would you choose this person to be in your lifeboat?*
> *If not, maybe it's time to sail without them."*

A "No" said gently with conviction is better for their life, and for yours, than a "yes" said only to please, or worse, to avoid strife. Unless you have the power to say no, you never really have the power to say yes.

But remember. When letting people go heed the words of the Dalai Lama:

"Be kind whenever possible. It is always possible."

Be ever spare with words. Words have more power to hurt or heal than daggers or bouquets. What comes out of your mouth is equally as important to a **Quiet Mind** as what you put into it. Here is the key. **If you would not write, and sign, and post in the social media what you are about to say, do not say it.**

If we spoke with only good to say, a hush would overtake society. Never judge, never blame, never scold. Retribution is but a reflection of our own character. Strive to leave everyone better than you found them. As Lao Tzu said in *Guide to the Virtuous Path* more than 2,000 years ago:

"Be kind to the good, be kind to the bad. Thus kindness multiplies."

The legendary Lao Tzu

14
Walk With Giants

It bears repeating many times. Befriend only those who are joyful and passionate and you will gradually shape yourself to them.

As Buddha said:

> *"Wisdom comes by cultivating the mind. Cultivating the mind comes by associating with positive people".*

If you want to do extraordinary things, you have to associate with extraordinary people. If you want to be able to express your potential there is nowhere else to go. Most information in the media, on the internet, and on television is distorted by hidden agendas, ignorance, and greed. Do not waste one day of your life on it.

As a consultant to three different Western governments, I have seen multiple versions of government announcements: the secret version for the policy makers, the version for the bureaucrats couched to best persuade them to follow the mandate, and the version for the public couched to confuse the opposition and upset as few voters as possible.

Often these versions are contradictory to each other. As a source of knowledge, the published forms are of little use. Public office compromises even the best of intellects. Government is far too difficult a task for the majority of politicians. As Barack Obama has said,

"What Washington needs is adult supervision."

Commercial prattle is even worse. The very literacy we need to use each day has become the biggest problem we face. Although the printed word used to be rightly prized as a source of knowledge ("It's in the book."), control over most of the information that flows into our heads has now completely disappeared. Various estimates indicate that about 90% of media, internet, and television information has no factual basis.

Be vigilant. Our seething commercial culture is always trying to trap you into unthinking reactions. Remember, it is NEVER the situation that counts, only what you think about it. Do not allow yourself to become as Earnest Hemingway said of the London crowds:

"Each one with his ha-penny newspaper intelligence."

One of the clearest examples of mass misinformation in North America is the two people out of every three who are seriously overweight, our biggest health problem. Humans are not naturally fat. To become fat, they have to be carefully misinformed.

Misinformation. All you get from most weight loss programs is the T-shirt.

Lack of leadership has allowed food manufacturers to distort our food so that it has turned most of us into fat-and-carbohydrate-processing factories to fill their bank accounts. And then, for the same commercial reasons, the same lack of leadership allows manufacturers to deny what they have done and preach continually that junk food is the epitome of nutrition.

This constant commercial misinformation is even more damaging to your mind. Why? Because everything you know, **EVERY SINGLE THING YOU KNOW**, you learned from someone else. We can understand the world and ourselves only to the limits of what we have learned from others.

Were you born into a different culture, you would speak a different language, have different beliefs, eat different foods, follow different customs, worship different gods. Yet they would be as real and true to you as every belief you now hold most dear.

Our whole consciousness is a construction built, bit by tiny bit, from what we have learned from others. You act as your knowledge tells you to act, and you learned it all from someone else. **The mind is a fertile garden. It will grow whatever you allow into its soil – flowers or weeds.**

Memorize the wisdom of Mahatma Gandhi to keep you on the right path to knowledge:

"Your beliefs become your thoughts. Your thoughts become your words. Your words become your actions. Your actions become your habits. Your habits become your values. Your values become your destiny."

"Generations to come will scarce believe that such a one as he ever in flesh and blood did walk upon this Earth." - Albert Einstein

The quality of your life is determined by the quality of your thought. Do not dilute your mind with the internet or media babble that renders many folk mere spectators of life, helpless to do anything. As renowned expert on language Mark Pagel says, *"The internet provides the perfect vehicle to teach humanity infinite stupidity"*.

Releasing the power of your brain is a lot more fun than net surfing or watching TV. Leadership guru Robin Sharma is fond of saying, *"Sell your TV; leaders have libraries."* Natural farmer and famous activist Joel Salatin suggests taking an axe to the TV. I couldn't go that far; I would miss *The Big Bang Theory*. But, I don't pretend it will expand my mind.

You are in control of your mind. Do not waste precious time spectating. Seize life by the tail and give it a good shaking every day. Just do it!

No, don't hesitate. Don't think, "I'll wait till I get this out of the way", or "When I finish that". **Your life cannot wait for the storm to pass. It's about learning to dance in the rain.**

"Sell your TV; leaders have libraries." - Robin Sharma

Qualify Your Advisors

Be careful what you learn because it becomes what you know. Personally qualify every professional you deal with before you let their advice into your brain. Examine your teachers carefully before you let them teach you anything.

Examine your doctors even more carefully before you ever let them examine you. There are many overweight doctors, for example, but no overweight good doctors. If they cannot control this eminently controllable risk to their own health, they do not know enough to look after yours.

If your dentist had bad teeth, would you let them fix yours? If a contractor's home is tumbledown, would you let them build yours? Accept information only from those who walk their talk, who are shining examples of what they profess to know.

Seek only the best. There are many folk with walls of academic degrees who pontificate on human cognition, as if it was less complicated than picking stocks or designing computer chips. On the contrary, your brain is the most complex matter we know, beside which the stock market is laughable simplicity, and computers quaint and cumbrous.

It takes a little reflection to realize just how complex our brains are. **From "shoes and ships and sealing wax" to internets and diamond rings, the human mind thought it all up from a planet of just sticks and rocks.**

Even the everyday science and technology we take for granted stems from the physics of elementary particles, way beyond the average comprehension. The underlying physics itself, without which most of modern technology would not exist, is beyond the comprehension of almost all of us.

Top thinkers make their knowledge available as simplified concepts, knowing well that understandable versions of their work will be inevitably misused by lesser minds. They persist anyway because they know it is only by educating the minds of others to greater thought that humanity advances from the savagery of the past. Seek top thinkers out and model yourself on them. Knowledge is and always has been the key that unlocks the power of the human brain.

Sir Tim Berners Lee and colleagues at CERN, the European Organization for Nuclear Research, invented the World Wide Web in the 1980s. Fully aware it would be shamelessly corrupted with nonsense and falsehood difficult to differentiate from knowledge, they still gave it to the world FREE OF CHARGE in 1989, simply to increase the global flow of knowledge. We are now in the throes of the biggest expansion of human knowledge since the invention of the printing press in the 15th century.

The best we can do to learn the right stuff is to walk with joyful giants. Associate with the work of people greater than you, and you will become greater. Allow your brain only the best information and you will expand your mind beyond your wildest dreams.

Throughout history all great leaders have been readers. Even Genghis Khan carried his library on an elephant as he went to war. Today we don't need the paper books or the elephant to carry them. We can carry Genghis Khan's whole library on our cell phone. What a blessing!

"No matter how busy you may think you are, you must find time for reading, or surrender yourself to self-chosen ignorance." - Confucius

Great books are rays of light to focus and direct the human mind. Make it a lifelong habit to read them every day.

Never think you have insufficient time or talent, or are too set in the wrong habits, or stuck in a senseless job. As leadership guru David Wood says, give yourself permission to be a disaster and go from there.

The past has no power over the present. Take what you have in this present moment as if it is the greatest choice you have made in your whole life. It's good to remember the deceptively simple wisdom of Dr. Seuss in *Oh, The Places You'll Go!*

"You have brains in your head. You have feet in your shoes.
You can steer yourself, any direction you choose!"

"Every Master was once a disaster." - Leadership guru David Wood

16
Become Your Greatest Thoughts

We sink as low as our lowest thoughts. Be ever alert to quell them. Avoid the uncharitable, the malicious, the cruel, the vengeful. Reject all evil thoughts from your mind. Wherever we walk with evil, grief shadows every step.

Remember the words of Buddha:

> *"Suffering follows an evil thought as the wheels of a cart follow the oxen that draw it."*

Reject all kinds of war, all kinds of violence. Reject any doctrine whose strength is an upraised stick. We have known it from Sun Tzu for millennia.

"The supreme art of war is to subdue the enemy
without fighting." - Sun Tzu, **The Art of War**

Civilization advances slowly. Less than a century ago America still sanctioned public hangings. 20,000 people came to see the last one, a 27-year-old murderer named Rainey Bathea, hanged in Kentucky in 1936.

When asked about that time what he thought of Western Civilization, Gandhi replied,

"I think it would be a good idea".

Public floggings and stoning to death are still common in barbaric countries, in stark contradiction to their clamor for world recognition as civilized. No surprise that countries whose governments sanction such violence are ever on the brink of war.

Suspect anyone who glorifies our blatant media thirst for retribution.

"Let he who is without sin cast the first stone." - John 8:7

Never mistake machismo for courage. Violence is always an act of weakness, driven by our primitive defensive emotions of the past. It is the answer of the coward.

Only the strong of mind have the courage to live without violence, without wars. We all have the power to develop this courage, but modern culture conditions us to believe that we cannot.

As Gandhi said:

"It makes no difference to the dead, the orphans or the homeless, whether the mad destruction of war is wrought under the name of terrorism, liberty, or democracy".

The world is full enough of hurts without violence to multiply them.

War is NEVER a path to peace. Peace IS the path. We have brain power to spare to follow that path. What we lack is the leadership.

Focus not on the faults of others, but on correcting your own faults. To advance on life's journey of joy, banish violence from your thoughts. **Wherever your life lacks love and compassion, therein lies your work.**

Echoing down the centuries from the greatest leaders the world has ever known, from Lao Tzu Confucius, Buddha, and Jesus, it bears repeating still. Do unto others as you would have them do unto you.

Quiet Mind allows us to take one further step. Gradually you will become able to *think* unto others as you would have them *think* unto you.

"Darkness cannot drive out darkness: only light can do that. Hate cannot drive out hate: only love can do that." - Martin Luther King

Your Greatest Thoughts

All that we are, all that we can be, is the result of what we have thought. We can grow only as great as our greatest thoughts.

Focus on the works of great leaders in all peaceful disciplines, people whom you admire. Doing so enables you to use the wisdom of the ages and advance rapidly on the journey of joy, rather than be limited to reinventing everything from scratch with merely your senses.

To the eye, for example, the world looks flat, and the sun and stars revolve around it. Without the successive contributions of Galileo, Kepler, Copernicus, and Newton from 1573-1726, we might still believe our eyes.

Before the invention of the printing press by Gutenberg in 1439, to spread written wisdom worldwide, a decade of our development today took more than a thousand years. Remains of humans with brains as large and complex as ours are now dated conclusively to 180,000 years ago. For almost 170,000 of those years, we were Stone Age hunter-gatherers, with little change in our top technology of chipping stones to make arrow and axe heads.

Symbolic communication by crude paintings on rocks began only about 30,000 years ago. Written language like the example shown on the next page began to appear in Ancient Egypt, Phoenicia, and the Indus civilization less than 10,000 years ago.

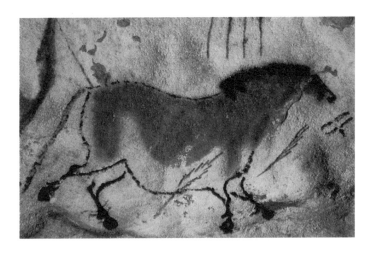

Cave painting from Lascaux, France,
Approximately 30,000 years old

Writing 5,500 years old on a pottery shard from Harappa, Pakistan.

About the same time written accounts of how to make bronze spread the new technology and ushered in the Bronze Age. Then about 3,500 years ago, the Greeks perfected the Phoenician alphabet and civilization was off to the races.

Without the development of written language, we would still be little ahead of grunting in the caves depicting animals in ochre on the walls. Now, since the inception of the internet in 1989, we are in the midst of the greatest wave of knowledge in human history.

This development of civilization emphasizes the writings of the great as the logical focus for life. **Use the written wisdom of the ages to construct your greatest thoughts. Then become them.**

Don't expect it to be easy. The path to wisdom is hard and steep. The Universe did not acknowledge any sense of obligation when Descartes first said, *"Cogito ergo sum"*.

But, little by little, you travel far.

A journey of a thousand miles begins with a single step. **Make every day of your life a creative act, like a never-ending work of art.**

It's tough to get going. Follow the advice of top business executive and star athlete Susan Sly. Do not try to do it alone. ***Link arms with joyful and passionate people who are on the same journey.*** You will progress farther and faster. One great source of contact with such folk is the company Isagenix®.

"Link arms with joyful and passionate people who are on the same journey." - Susan Sly

17
Love

The greatest thought you can become is love. Though she lived among the starving beggars in Calcutta, Mother Teresa said,

"There is greater hunger in the world for love than for bread."

Oftentimes we confuse love with acquisition. Every greedy business day millions of advertisements misuse the word "love" to praise their wares. Of course we take pleasure in beautiful things, but there is no love in them. A diamond is just a lifeless stone.

Mother Teresa

USA

2010

"There is greater hunger in the world for love than for bread."

Be they fashioned more majestic than the Taj Mahal, bricks and mortar sing not one loving note. You cannot give love to a house, a car, a picture on the wall. Love is an exchange of joy between you and another living soul.

Do not seek love without. All the love there is waits inside you. You have to find it step by step. Seek within. You alone know when your feet take up the path. You alone know when your love or lack of it makes you feel good or ill.

"Love is always patient, always kind. Love does not envy, does not boast. Love does not take offence, nor hold resent. Love does not seek return but always trusts, always hopes, always endures, always."
- 1 Corinthians 13:4-8 (modern translation)

"Love is not love which alters when it alteration finds
Nor bends with the remover to remove
Oh no, it is an ever fixed mark
That looks on tempests and is never shaken."
- Sonnet 116, William Shakespeare

The flow of love does not turn on and off. It becomes the constant stream of every day. Waste not one day without loving because time is the measure of your span. Give all the love you have each day as if it is your last.

You will be hurt. But the hurts are most reflections of our own faults. As Mother Teresa advises, love more until you rise above the hurt:

"Despite giving your best to the world, you may be kicked
in the teeth. Give the best you've got anyway. What else
is there to do?" - Mother Teresa

Although he was kicked many times during 27 years in prison, when Nelson Mandela became President of South Africa, he answered the cruelty only with love and forgiveness.

"As I walked out the door toward the gate that would lead to my freedom, I knew if I didn't leave my bitterness and hatred behind, I'd still be in prison."

As you grow your loving heart you will come to see that love does not possess. It is an unconditional gift, not a contract.

In *The Prophet*, Khalil Gibran reminds us:

"Love gives naught but itself
And takes naught but from itself.
It possesses not, nor would it be possessed."

Khalil Gibran

Love is not lust, although lust comes in very handy when the day has proven glum. Love consists less of gazing into your lover's eyes, and more of looking forward in the same direction together.

To have a true beloved, you must find the path to love in your heart. Hold steadfast to it. Use it every day to laugh easily, love deeply, kiss slowly, like it's the first kiss and the last kiss. Forgive quickly. Forgive everyone and everything. In return you get life's greatest gift of joy.

Hold tight to the hand of your beloved. Weak and mortal as we are, the touch of love gives courage to keep us on the path.

"A Book of Verse beneath the Bough,
A Jug of Wine, a Loaf of Bread, and Thou
Beside me singing in the Wilderness
And Wilderness be Paradise enow!"

- Rubaiyat of Omar Khayyam

Make no mistake; love is your richest possession. It is free and inexhaustible good. It never diminishes. The more we give the more love multiplies.

Over time, love wakes within us a beautiful stranger whose existence we had never suspected. To love every day is to be gradually reborn.

Each day we act with unconditional love, we advance upon the journey of joy. As our joy of life increases, we increase the joy of everyone around us.

There are many layers concealing the love within your heart, and the bud of it will be coarse, and covered with the grime of past emotional distress. But, as you penetrate within, the grime will fall away. Each succeeding layer will bring you closer to the purity that waits in each of us. Be patient, for the cup fills slowly, drop by drop.

Few of us come to do great deeds for humankind, but all of us can do small deeds, each day, with joyous love. By far the greatest growth of civilization has come from innumerable little acts of love.

If you would change things for good in your life and in the world, then you must become the change you seek. Not the elements of fire or storm, or pestilence, or even death, can erase deeds done with a loving heart.

Follow Mother Teresa's advice and seek the silent sounds of Nature to clarify your thought. Whatever you think clearly enough, so you will become. Shape your thoughts towards selflessness, and joy will flow through you as a river, shine from you as a beacon.

Adopt **Quiet Mind** and join me on the journey to perfect your capacity for the joyous emotions of love and compassion. Achieve your unique and bountiful future in this endless adventure of life, midst the beauty and growth and rhythms of Nature, in trees and mountains and oceans, and the perpetual rising of the sun.

"Truth cannot be found in noise and restlessness. Truth is found in silence. See how nature—trees, flowers, grass—grows in silence; see the stars, the moon and the sun, how they move in silence... We need silence to be able to touch the truth."
- Mother Teresa

Alive

Flee fast the ordinary
Of every day.
Reject the counsel
Of the prudent and the sane.

Feel for the pulse of your heart.
Seek out those souls
Who animate its passion.
Cultivate those labors
That quicken its beat,
And count only little the cost.

For life without risk,
Without trembling emotion,
Crescendos of triumph,
Despairs of defeat,
Lets the bondage of commonplace
Bind you spectator,
Condemned but to watching
The living of others
Who dance with the fire of a passionate heart.

- Michael Colgan